Chapter 1

PILGRIMS
TOGETHER

1828	1837	1848	1850	1858
United Rhine Mission Society formed in Germany	German mission society sends John Muehlhaeuser to serve in North America	Muehlhaeuser moves from New York to Wisconsin	First meeting of the new Wisconsin Synod at Granville church with Muehlhaeuser as president	Synod numbers: 17 pastors 16 parish schools 7 Sunday schools 3 teachers

LET'S BEGIN THE STORY

History is the story of people. All of us remember our own histories. We review old pictures and remember. Every family has its own history too. When family members gather for birthdays, weddings, and funerals, they retell important events and experiences that shaped the individuals and the family. This little history is a retelling of such events and experiences.

Through the gospel God has gathered us into his family. As members of his family, we rehearse how the Lord of the church has gathered us together and made us what we are. We know that all events are in the hands of a gracious and loving God. He controls even the hard, difficult, and tragic stories so that they serve his gracious, good purposes.

This history of the Wisconsin Evangelical Lutheran Synod (WELS) is a collection of stories about God's work in the hearts of those who have gone before us. Their stories are often much like the stories of our own lives, filled more with struggles than glorious triumphs. Yet, through all the struggles, the Lord of the church watched over the synod's founders and led them forward. It is, therefore, more a story of God's grace and power than of human achievement. We tell this story to confess that God has shaped us through the events and personalities of the past. As we retell the story, we also remember that God continues to shape us to be his people—his witnesses—in our world.

THE ROOTS

Settlers from Germany came to the United States to begin a new life. Large numbers of them settled in Michigan, Minnesota, and Wisconsin. Many had Lutheran roots. Those who remained in Germany saw an opportunity to do mission work in the new world. One man, Christian Friedrich Spittler, had a hand in founding two mission schools—one in Basel, another at St. Chrischona. The St. Chrischona school was called the Pilgrims' Mission and, together with the school at Basel, sent men to serve the Germans in the new world. Some of these men later became important to the history of the Wisconsin Synod.

A third mission school had an even more important part in our history. In 1828 Christians in a cluster of German towns along the Rhine formed the United Rhine Mission Society. They established a mission school in Barmen. One student of that school was John Muehlhaeuser. In 1837 the *Langenberger Verein*, which was a division of the united mission society, sent him to North America with the desire that his service "may redound to the eternal salvation of many souls."

John Muehlhaeuser arrived on October 3, 1837, and served as the pastor of a group of Lutherans in Rochester, New York, for ten years. In 1846 Pastor Muehlhaeuser met the boat that brought two new men from the Barmen mission school—John Weinmann and William Wrede. The mission society had sent John Weinmann to the Milwaukee area in answer to a request by a layman for a pastor in Town Oakwood. William Wrede, the other man the mission society sent to America, began his work in Callicoon, New York. But in 1849 he moved to Wisconsin to serve the congregation at Granville, near Milwaukee.

Pastor John Muehlhaeuser

After Weinmann began his work in Wisconsin, he reported to Muehlhaeuser of the many Germans there who had no pastor. In 1848 John Muehlhaeuser resigned from his duties in Rochester in order to carry out mission work in Wisconsin. He wrote, "I served the Evangelical Lutheran Church at Rochester ten years. Since the congregation was well established and capable of providing for a pastor adequately and I was still feeling healthy and strong, yes, especially prompted by Pastor Weinmann, I resolved to move with my family to Wisconsin so that I could still carry out mission work for some years."

TOGETHER IN WISCONSIN

When these men arrived in Wisconsin, they did not fit in with other Lutherans. Two other Lutheran synods already had congregations in the Milwaukee area, but Muehlhaeuser, Weinmann, and Wrede had come from a mission school that served both Lutherans and the Reformed. Their school minimized the differences in doctrine. John Muehlhaeuser wrote, "I am in a position to offer every child of God and servant of Christ the hand of fellowship over the denominational fence." These men were neither strictly Lutheran nor strictly Reformed. The confessional Lutherans in Milwaukee would not accept men who claimed to be Lutheran and yet tolerated the doctrines of the Reformed.

In December of 1849, Weinmann, Wrede, and Paul Meiss, who also had Barmen ties, met in the parish hall of Grace Church with John Muehlhaeuser to discuss founding a new Lutheran synod. The group resolved to form a synod in Wisconsin, which it called the First German Evangelical Lutheran Synod of Wisconsin. It chose John Muehlhaeuser as its president and decided to meet on May 26, 1850, in Granville to review the constitution that its new president was to write. On that day the four men were joined by Kaspar Pluess of Slinger and held the first meeting of the new synod.

The constitution stated clearly that these men desired to be Lutheran. It required new pastoral candidates to pledge themselves to the Unaltered Augsburg Confession and the other Confessions of the Evangelical Lutheran Church. Yet some time after the meeting, the reference to the Lutheran Confessions was crossed out in the original manuscript and the words "pure Bible Christianity" and "pure Bible Word" were written above it. In those early days, the Wisconsin Synod was not an example of clarity or conviction.

TOGETHER IN MICHIGAN

What about the Germans who had settled in other parts of the Midwest? In 1833 the mission society in Basel,

Pastor Friedrich Schmid

Germany, sent Friedrich Schmid to serve German settlers in the Ann Arbor area in Michigan. He established a number of preaching stations during his first 10 years in Michigan. In 1842 or 1843, he founded the Mission Synod in order to share the gospel with others, including the Amercian Indians. But difficulty over what it meant to be Lutheran was one factor that caused the Mission Synod to disband in 1848.

After 12 years, two more men from the Basel mission society arrived in Michigan. On December 10 and 11 in 1860, eight pastors with their delegates met in Detroit to found the Michigan Synod. The new synod pledged itself "to all the canonical books of Holy Scripture as the sole rule and norm of its faith and life; also to all the symbolical books of our Evangelical Lutheran Church as the true interpretation of Holy Scripture." Progress for the new synod was slow because of the lack of faithful pastors. In 1868 the Michigan Synod numbered 3,300; ten years later it only numbered 3,350.

TOGETHER IN MINNESOTA

Scandinavian Lutherans arrived in Minnesota before the German Lutherans. In 1854 Pastor Erland Carlsson from Chicago organized three

Granville Church Splits: Reformed and Lutheran

On Christmas Day in 1847, a group of Lutheran and Reformed families formed the German Evangelical Lutheran and Reformed Church of Granville Township. The group of 20 German families held services without a church building or a pastor for seven months. Two pastors served the congregation for a short time; one of them was relieved of his duties because of his doctrine and practice.

On June 17, 1849, the families dedicated a church made of logs. Pastors Muehlhaeuser and Weinmann attended the dedication service. About six months later, Pastor Wrede became pastor of the group and worked to move the congregation closer to sound Lutheran doctrine. On May 26, 1850, the Granville church became the site of the first meeting of the new Wisconsin Synod.

During the next ten years, the congregation gradually became more and more Lutheran. While it was still worshiping in the log church, the Reformed branch of the congregation formed the West Granville Presbyterian Church and built a church across the street. The remaining Lutherans came to be known as Salem Evangelical Lutheran Church and built what has become the landmark church of the WELS. Both the landmark church and the Presbyterian church across the street still stand on north 107th Street in Milwaukee.

Swedish Lutheran congregations in the Minnesota territory. The East Pennsylvania Synod sent Pastor J. C. F. Heyer to begin an English-speaking mission in the Twin Cities. Heyer had just returned from mission work in India. He was the first Lutheran missionary from the United States to serve in a foreign mission.

Pastor J. C. F. Heyer

Pastor Heyer began serving the English- speaking Lutherans and gathering the German-speaking ones. He sought to forge a union of German and Scandinavian congregations, but the effort failed when the Scandinavians formed their own synod, the Augustana Synod. Heyer then concentrated on bringing the German- and English-speaking congregations together. In 1860 six pastors met to found the Minnesota Synod.

A LOOK BACK AT THE BEGINNING

In those early years, two problems faced these young church bodies. First, they suffered from a lack of dedicated and committed Lutheran pastors. They depended on the mission societies in Germany for their pastors, but the mission societies had many requests for pastors and could not supply all that the German settlers needed. Second, the mission work was difficult. In order to gather people together, the early mission workers often chose to join with other Protestants, especially the Reformed. For them, it was a compromise that put practical matters ahead of God's truth. Yet, as lax as they were, they had the desire to be faithful to the Scriptures and confess the Lutheran faith. Over time their commitment grew until they no longer compromised the truth. From these weak beginnings, God grew a church body that would be willing to follow the truth of God's Word no matter what the costs.

Chapter 2

GROWING STRONGER TOGETHER

More Conviction and Faithfulness

Still Not Enough Pastors

Worship Then and Now

Untangled and Lutheran

Minnesota and Wisconsin Synods Move Closer

Another Step Closer Together in Christ

Together with Others in Christ: The Synodical Conference

Life in Wisconsin: 1871

1860	1865	1868	1871	1872
John Bading becomes new synod president	Seminary building dedicated in Watertown synod periodical *Gemeinde-Blatt* appears	Synod severs ties with Germany to become more Lutheran	Minnesota Synod withdraws from General Council and moves to closer ties with Wisconsin Synod	Ohio, Missouri, Norwegian, Wisconsin, Illinois, and Minnesota Synods hold first convention of Synodical Conference

More Conviction and Faithfulness

In 1860 the Wisconsin Synod numbered 20 pastors, 48 congregations, 23 parish schools, and 20 Sunday schools. That year President Muehlhaeuser declined to serve as president because of advancing age and because the burdens of his office were "becoming more pressing year by year." The convention granted him the honorary title "Senior" with the privilege of sitting at the presiding officer's right.

The new president was John Bading. Muehlhaeuser might have viewed the Confessions as "paper fences," but Bading did not. To him they proclaimed the truth of God's Word for every age. In his address to the 1861 convention, President Bading encouraged the synod to be willing to sacrifice "good and blood, life and limb and rather suffer all than depart one hair's breath from the truth we have learned." The next year he reminded the synod that they "were all pledged to the Confessions of our church and indeed not *in so far as* but *because* they agree with God's Word." He expressed a sentiment that was shared by a growing number of others in the new synod.

Still Not Enough Pastors

As important as this shift was, the synod still lacked an adequate supply of pastors for its congregations. Pastors still came from the mission societies in Germany, but only a few new pastors arrived each year. Without a supply of faithful pastors, congregations suffered from intruders who had little training, relying instead on glib tongues and pleasant personalities. One congregation's first pastor turned out to be a Methodist, and the second was a converted Catholic priest!

To overcome the problem, the synod decided in 1863 to establish its own seminary in Watertown. Actually the school was to be a combination seminary, college, and high school—a kind of university.

Worship Then and Now

Mrs. Viola Klinger, a lifelong member of Salem in Milwaukee, remembers how different attending church was years ago.

The church had two aisles. A low partition separated one set of pews from the other. The men sat on the right, and the women and children sat on the left. The men went to Communion first. When they were all finished, the women would hand the babies across the partition for the men to hold while the women went to Communion. Separation of the men and women continued in many churches for many years.

The congregation sang German hymns from a small hymnal that had no music. And the organ may have been a reed organ that the organist had to pump.

Today Lutheran families sit together and sing in English. Parents with small children may sit in the rear of the church. When they go to Communion, some attend together and carry their children with them to the Lord's Table. Other parents split the task of caring for their small children. One parent will attend while the other cares for the children, waiting to attend later.

The austere worship of years ago has changed, but Lutherans still worship the same Lord Jesus. He has not changed, but so much has changed in every congregation. Some congregations did not have stained-glass windows at first. Now stained-glass windows, electric lighting, sound systems, powerful organs, bell choirs, a new hymnal, and carpets all add to contemporary worship.

The school first had the name Wisconsin University. Later the name became Northwestern University, and in 1910 it became Northwestern College.

Building a new school was a great step forward, but in 1863 the synod had no money to build. In the fall of that year, the seminary began in a private home with one professor, Edward Moldehnke. The synod hoped to solve its lack of funds for building by sending President Bading to Germany and Russia on a fund-raising mission. Bading's initial success abroad encouraged the synod to begin building the new seminary. A building was dedicated in September of 1865.

UNTANGLED AND LUTHERAN

These steps did not immediately solve the problem of manpower for the Wisconsin Synod. But they were important because they moved the synod toward greater independence. The desire to have faithful Lutheran pastors began the process of untangling the Lutherans in Wisconsin from the mission societies in Germany.

The mission societies provided pastors to serve Lutherans and the Reformed in the new world and also provided money for a traveling missionary. In addition, President Bading had sought and received a substantial amount of money for the school in Watertown—over $10,000 was sent back to Wisconsin. An additional $7,500 was held in Prussia in the form of endowment funds. In spite of their help to the Lutherans in Wisconsin, the mission societies were still promoting union between Lutherans and the Reformed. For churches that desired to be more Lutheran, that situation presented a rather awkward problem. Soon it became evident that ties with the mission societies could not continue.

The 1867 convention of the Wisconsin Synod discussed the issue of union. One report suggested that the union of Lutherans and Reformed promoted by the Prussian government was a "misuse of the power of the state over the church" and enslaved consciences. A milder report was adopted. But when the mission societies heard the report, they protested. In 1868 the synod thanked the mission societies for their past gifts but did not change its mind, and the young synod severed ties with Germany. The action came at a price. The Berlin mission societies did not release the $7,500 held in Prussia or send any more workers to Wisconsin.

The 1868 convention also sought closer ties with the Lutheran Church—Missouri Synod (LCMS) and passed an important resolution. The delegates resolved that the synod, "with the whole orthodox Lutheran Church rejects each and every altar and pulpit fellowship with those that believe falsely or otherwise as contradictory to the doctrine and practice of the Lutheran Church." In just a few short years, the Wisconsin Synod had grown more Lutheran and closer together in Christ. It turned away from an entanglement with those who taught and practiced what was contrary to the Scriptures and the Lutheran Confessions. At the same time, the synod reached out to those who taught and practiced the truth.

MINNESOTA AND WISCONSIN SYNODS MOVE CLOSER

The Lutherans in the Minnesota Synod wanted closer ties to the Lutherans in the Wisconsin Synod. President Heyer had visited the Wisconsin Synod convention in 1863, and President Bading and Professor Hoenecke attended the Minnesota Synod convention in 1869. They offered a proposal for the federation of the two synods. The doctrinal commissions of both synods met in La Crosse, Wisconsin, and declared that there was real unity—both synods adhered to the same doctrines. But one obstacle remained. The Minnesota Synod still belonged to the General Council, which was promoting a vague Lutheranism. Wisconsin had already withdrawn from the General Council. Pastor Sieker, the new president of the Minnesota Synod, led the Minnesota Lutherans to confess that

Lutheran altars are for Lutheran Christians and Lutheran pulpits only for Lutheran preachers. In 1871 the Minnesota Synod withdrew from the General Council and moved to closer ties with the Wisconsin Synod.

The agreement between the synods opened the doors of Northwestern University in Watertown to students from Minnesota who desired training as pastors. In addition, the Minnesota Synod became a partner in producing the Wisconsin Synod's periodical, *Gemeinde-Blatt*. This church paper had appeared for the first time on September 1, 1865, and was intended to instruct the members of the Wisconsin Synod congregations in doctrine and practice.

ANOTHER STEP CLOSER TOGETHER IN CHRIST

President Bading

The delegates to the 1868 Wisconsin Synod convention in Racine declared that they knew of no differences that would keep the Wisconsin and Missouri Synods apart. The convention instructed President Bading to take the "proper steps to bring about peace so that there might be mutual recognition as Lutheran synods and brotherly relations between members of both synods in the spirit of truth on the basis of pure doctrine." On the day the Racine convention closed, President Bading presented the Wisconsin Synod's decisions to the Northern District of the Missouri Synod, which was meeting in Milwaukee.

A discussion between representatives of both synods took place in Milwaukee in October of 1868. In the past, President Walther of the Missouri Synod had criticized the Wisconsin Synod for its brand of vague Lutheranism. It was necessary to demonstrate that things had changed in Wisconsin. After the meeting in Milwaukee, President

Walther reported, "All our reservations about...Wisconsin...have been put to shame." Both synods ratified the agreement in their conventions the next year, 1869.

TOGETHER WITH OTHERS IN CHRIST: THE SYNODICAL CONFERENCE

At the end of the 1860s, a number of independent synods would not join the General Council at all because the Council did not commit itself fully in doctrine and practice to confessional Lutheranism. They were the Ohio, Missouri, and Norwegian Synods. Others had joined and later withdrew. They were the Wisconsin, Minnesota, and Illinois Synods. In 1870 the Ohio Synod resolved to take steps "towards effecting a proper understanding between the synods of Missouri, of Wisconsin, of Illinois, and our own synod, which all occupy substantially the same position, and arranging a plan of cooperation in the work of the Lord."

Things happened quickly after that. In January of 1871, representatives of four synods (Ohio, Missouri, Norwegian, and Wisconsin) met in Chicago. The conference set to work on a proposed Synodical Conference constitution and discussed possible joint efforts in training workers. Another meeting took place in Fort Wayne in November at which the Illinois and Minnesota Synods were represented. All was ready for the birth of the Synodical Conference.

In July of 1872 the first convention of the Synodical Conference was held at St. John's Church in Milwaukee, President Bading's church. Professor Walther preached the opening sermon. "O blessed and blissful day!" Walther said. Lutherans had come together because they shared a full commitment to the Holy Scriptures and to all the doctrines of the Lutheran Confessions. In addition, their confession was more than just words; their practice matched their confession.

LIFE IN WISCONSIN: 1871

Pastor J. Meyer began his ministry in Wisconsin in 1871. In February he wrote to his fiancée, Meta Hebnken, who was still in Germany. Here are some excerpts:

My Beloved Meta!

You perhaps are becoming impatient and dissatisfied about my long silence.…I must heartily beg your pardon.

Winchester lies in the woods so that I rightly call myself a bush preacher.…My house is a log house, built of large blocks of wood, but there are nevertheless several rooms in it.…Besides the house I also have a barn in which there is a place also for a cow and horse and a woodshed.

The church is close to the house, but it looks deplorable, just like a sheep barn over there, but I will soon get a better one, for next summer something new is to be built. Besides this congregation I have three others and may get a fourth on top of it, so that I will have five churches where I must preach.…So you see here in America one has to travel about and besides has to be everything,

pastor, schoolteacher, and janitor. That is why you must excuse me if it takes longer for me to get at writing.

I do not have time to keep house as a bachelor. Therefore, I beg you, hurry as much as possible to come here. But I would like to ask one more thing: how is your sewing skill? When you are here, you will have to make everything yourself, your clothes and also my pants and vests for these things are too expensive here. If one wants to have pants or vest made, it costs about two dollars for labor and that much a bush pastor does not earn here. So learn as much as possible about sewing.…

Today I started confirmation instructions.…The children here are so very stupid, so that they don't know anything at all. Many can't even read properly as yet.…

With warm greetings I remain your ever loving, J. Meyer.

Chapter 3

WORKING TOGETHER

A Desire to Walk Alone

Three Synods Build Training Schools

A Closer Walk Together

Reaction in Michigan

Mission to a "Foreign" Nation

1866	1878	1892	1893	1914
J. M. Hoeckendorf's congregation of 125 Lutherans moves to Nebraska	*Relocated seminary begins at 13th and Vine in Milwaukee with six students*	*Michigan, Minnesota, and Wisconsin Synods form federation called Evangelical Lutheran Joint Synod of Wisconsin and Other States*	*Federation adopts Apache mission effort as its world mission project*	*English Northwestern Lutheran begins publication*

A Desire to Walk Alone

On May 23, 1866, a group of 125 Lutherans
set out from Ixonia, Wisconsin, on its way to
Nebraska. They traveled in 53 ox-drawn
covered wagons with a herd of cattle and a
flock of sheep. They wanted peace; they had

had enough religious bickering and fighting, especially the
bickering among the Lutherans in southeastern Wisconsin. In one case a
Lutheran teacher from Lebanon, Wisconsin, was excommunicated for
refusing to admit he had sinned by playing popular tunes on his violin.

These people were convinced that all the bickering came about because
of the synods. They wanted to get away from synods so they could
worship God without the squabbling. Their pastor, J. M. Hoeckendorf,
had even traveled to Chicago to object to the founding of the Missouri
Synod in 1847. He did not want anything to do with synods, and his
congregation agreed with him.

So his congregation left Wisconsin and moved to Nebraska. Along the way
they stopped every Sunday morning for worship. After almost two months,
they arrived at the place near Norfolk that a scouting party had selected
earlier. Pastor Hoeckendorf came to Nebraska to serve them the next year.

The plan worked well, at least for a time. Pastor Hoeckendorf trained
his son to become the next pastor of the group. Everything seemed to
be working as planned. Unfortunately, his son died shortly before he
was to be ordained and installed. Heartbroken, the father died soon
afterwards. Without a pastor these Lutheran Christians were like sheep
without a shepherd, and something had to be done.

Some of the members had heard of Professor Ernst of Northwestern
University in Watertown, Wisconsin, and invited him to Norfolk to

advise them. The elders of the church examined Ernst's theology before allowing him to speak. When he did speak, Ernst advised the congregation to call Michael Pankow, a graduate of the Missouri Synod's Springfield seminary. It did, but at the time, the Nebraska Lutherans did not join the Wisconsin Synod, even though their new pastor did. Over the years the Nebraska Lutherans expanded their mission work into Iowa, Colorado, and South Dakota. In 1904 they joined the federation that the Wisconsin Synod had joined in 1892.

THREE SYNODS BUILD TRAINING SCHOOLS

The deaths of Pastor Hoeckendorf and his son underscored one reason why Lutheran Christians came together. They needed pastors for their churches and teachers for their schools. Every new generation of Christians needs a new generation of called workers. Larger church bodies—both Lutheran and others—had schools to train pastors and teachers, and the Wisconsin Synod recognized the need too. In 1863 it began its seminary in Watertown. In 1865 it established a college in the same city.

When the Wisconsin Synod established ties with the Missouri Synod, it moved its seminary program to St. Louis. Then at the convention in 1877 the Wisconsin Synod resolved to bring its seminary back to Wisconsin. The next year three seminary professors, Adolf Hoenecke, Eugene Notz, and August Graebner, began the relocated seminary at 13th and Vine in Milwaukee with six students. Over the next few years, more than one hundred seminary students graduated to serve Wisconsin Synod congregations.

The Minnesota Synod recognized the need for workers too. One of its arrangements with the Wisconsin Synod was to train its future pastors at Northwestern in Watertown. The Minnesota Synod was to call its own professor and to contribute annually for his support. Unfortunately at its convention in 1875, the Minnesota Synod asked for a delay in the payment. For two summers plagues of grasshoppers had destroyed the state's harvests, and the Minnesota Synod could not raise the necessary funds. Besides, its students had turned to Springfield instead of Watertown for their seminary training.

The Minnesota Synod, in spite of its relationship with its sister synod to the east, resolved to build its own worker-training school. At its convention in 1883, it stipulated that part of the money should be collected before construction began and that all congregations should be granted an opportunity to propose a site for the college. President C. J. Albrecht and his New Ulm congregation chose to ignore the stipulations. In 1884 the convention delegates were faced with a building already going up on the bluffs overlooking New Ulm.

In 1860 the Michigan Synod felt the same need for future pastors and teachers. Pastor Eberhardt, one of the founding fathers of the Michigan Synod, succeeded in convincing his synod of the need for a seminary to train pastors. In 1885 the Michigan Lutherans established Michigan Lutheran Seminary at Manchester. In 1887 the school moved to Saginaw. By 1892 it had supplied 12 pastors to Michigan congregations. But 1892 brought changes to all three Midwestern synods.

A CLOSER WALK TOGETHER

President Lederer of the Michigan Synod paid a visit to President Albrecht of the Minnesota Synod in New Ulm. The two presidents discussed plans for an association of their synods with the Wisconsin

Synod. In August of 1891, a preliminary meeting was held in Watertown. The fall pastoral conferences of the three synods heard the preliminary plan and agreed with it. Then the 1892 conventions of all three synods adopted the proposals for the federation and gave the presidents the power to set a date for the first convention of the federation.

The three synods—Michigan, Minnesota, and Wisconsin—formed the federation officially on October 11–13, 1892, in Milwaukee at St. John's Church. The official title of the federation was the Evangelical Lutheran Joint Synod of Wisconsin and Other States. In 1892 it was a federation of only Wisconsin, Michigan, and Minnesota. The three synods joined because they shared the same beliefs and because they wanted to work together more efficiently.

The federation set three general areas of cooperation. First, it agreed to put out "a common church periodical, a theological journal, a school journal, and an annual." The *Gemeinde-Blatt* served as the church periodical and another periodical called the *Schulzeitung* became the federation's school journal. The theological journal came later. The first issue of the *Theologische Quartalschrift* appeared in 1904.

The second area of cooperation was missions. Two important steps were taken at this time. Home missions became the responsibility of each synod, but the home mission effort came "under the supervision of the federation, which will allocate men and monies available for this purpose."

A group photo was a common practice at synod conventions.

World missions were fully the responsibility of the federation. The 1893 convention of the federation adopted the Apache mission effort as its world mission project.

The third cooperative effort was in training workers. The educational proposals set a theological seminary in Wisconsin. Plans had been approved for a new and larger seminary building at 60th and Lloyd in Wauwatosa. The cornerstone for the new seminary was laid in a special service on October 13, 1892, the closing day of the federation's founding convention. In addition to the seminary in Wauwatosa, the federation continued the college and preparatory school in Watertown. It chose the college in New Ulm as its teachers college and included a preparatory school there. The seminary of the Michigan Synod was changed dramatically. The federation discontinued the theological department and made it a preparatory school.

REACTION IN MICHIGAN

Not everyone in Michigan wanted a federation, and many were not pleased when the federation changed their seminary to a preparatory school. The Michigan Synod protested the change, and the federation agreed to leave the issue in the hands of the Michigan Synod for resolution. Soon several protesters launched a "save the seminary" campaign. The conflict resulted in a split in the Michigan Synod, some siding with the federation and others opposing it. The Michigan Synod actually withdrew from the federation in 1896. Those who remained with the federation became the Michigan District Synod of the federation.

The school, caught in the middle of the conflict, suffered. It had only one student in 1907, the year the Michigan Lutheran Seminary in Saginaw closed. Only Mrs. May, the housekeeper and caretaker, remained, but the school did reopen. In 1909 the Michigan Synod chose to rejoin the federation and then reopened its school as a preparatory school in 1910, retaining its name, Michigan Lutheran Seminary. The conflict had been healed.

MISSION TO A "FOREIGN" NATION

In the fall of 1892, the Wisconsin federation sent out two scouts to find an American Indian mission field that no other church bodies had entered. A Presbyterian missionary directed them to the Apache nation in Arizona. In the following year, the work began at Peridot, near the San Carlos River.

Over the years several faithful missionaries have shared the gospel with the Apache nation. Missionary pioneers include Gustav Harders, who spent 12 years in Arizona after leaving Jerusalem Lutheran Church in Milwaukee. He wrote three novels with American Indian settings, *Jaalahn*, *La Paloma*, and *Dohaschtida*. E. E. Guenther came to the Apaches with his bride in 1911. Because he was tall, the Apaches called him *Inashood N'daesn*, the Long One. These missionaries spent their lives sharing the gospel in Arizona. Names like Rosin and Uplegger are also included in the roster of those who have served.

For many years the federation's work among the Apaches was the most persistent outreach mission to a "foreign" people. At the time some expressed misgivings about conducting world mission work. They suggested that "world missions is not an essential work of a church body." The other work faced by the federation seemed to indicate that world missions was not a significant priority. Over the years this attitude has changed, but at the time it influenced the work of the federation among the Apache nation and explains why the work among the Apaches seemed to be the only "foreign" work for so long.

Dr. Francis Uplegger developed an Apache alphabet and translated many religious materials into what had been only a spoken language.

Chapter 4

ONE IN
FAITH

Searching the Scriptures

Closer Together: 1917

A Merger: Working Together

World War I and the Depression

*World War I Calls
WELS Members to War*

Searching the Scriptures

The small group of Lutheran Christians that had gathered at the Granville church in 1850 had changed. It was no longer vaguely Lutheran; now it was committed to the Scriptures and the Lutheran Confessions. In growing more Lutheran, it had found others who believed as it did. The Wisconsin Synod had developed ties with the Lutheran Church—Missouri Synod and helped found the Synodical

Professor Hoenecke

Conference. The Minnesota and Michigan Synods shared the faith of their Wisconsin and Missouri counterparts and drew closer together in a federation with Wisconsin.

Professor Pieper

Professor Schaller

One of the most significant steps the federation took in 1892 was establishing a joint seminary in Wauwatosa, Wisconsin. Controversies over the teachings of the Bible continued to arise not only in our own church and the other Lutheran churches but also in the larger Christian world. Over the years the faculty at Wauwatosa provided the leadership that kept the federation and its successor faithful to the Bible's

teachings. Some of the controversies and differences included teachings on church, ministry, election, conversion, justification, and fellowship.

The Wisconsin Synod became known for the approach of its Wauwatosa faculty. In the midst of controversy, the faculty went back to the Scriptures to discover what God revealed in his Word. When they discovered what the Scriptures revealed, they held to it firmly and without compromise. Their approach became known as the Wauwatosa Theology or the Wauwatosa Gospel. That term still describes the approach of the seminary faculty.

Such men as Adolf Hoenecke, August Pieper, J. P. Koehler, and John Schaller played significant roles in leading the synod through the controversies of the first 25 years of the 20th century. Adolf Hoenecke had more to do with earlier doctrinal controversies. Yet when he died in 1908, his influence lingered in the approach and thinking of the others. Much of their writing was published in German in the *Theologische Quartalschrift*, which began publication in 1904. Some of their writings have been translated and published in a multivolume set of books entitled *The Wauwatosa Theology*.

CLOSER TOGETHER: 1917

The synods that made up the Wisconsin federation and those that made up the Synodical Conference steered away from the doctrinal confusion that appeared in other Lutheran synods at the time. Other Lutheran bodies came together too. Three Norwegian Lutheran churches merged into the Evangelical Lutheran Church (ELC). In 1918 several large Lutheran bodies joined together in the United Lutheran Church in America (ULCA). But, for the most part, these mergers represented church bodies that were joined together without agreeing on the teachings of the Bible.

On the other hand, the members of the Synodical Conference maintained that there could be no real unity without agreement on the doctrines of the Bible. Again and again our forefathers had to study Scripture and confess their belief in its truth. They readily joined with those who shared their beliefs but avoided union with those who confessed different doctrines.

Points of doctrine are not minor theological hairsplitting. The issues raised in the church, from the earliest days of the apostles down to our own, involve what God reveals in the Bible and wants us to believe. For example, when the doctrine of justification was called into question by other Lutherans, August Pieper responded, "One cannot oppose any doctrine of God's Word with impunity...But whoever molests the doctrine of justification stabs the gospel in the heart and is on the way of losing entirely Christian doctrine and personal faith and of falling into the arms of heathenism."

By 1917 the three synods of Wisconsin, Minnesota, and Michigan had been joined by the Nebraska Synod (1904). All four of the separate synods shared the same commitment to the truth of the Bible. Since no doctrinal divisions existed among the four synods, it was a natural step to merge into a single body. In addition, the federation's cooperative efforts in publication, worker-training, and missions had proved to be so successful that greater coordination promised even more effective work. What better way to celebrate the four hundreth anniversary of Luther's Ninety-five Theses than with a merger. It was an opportunity to celebrate Lutheran roots and real unity in Christ's truth. By comparison to many mergers among other Lutherans at the time, this one was small. The 1919 statistics list the merged Wisconsin Synod to be about 127,000 communicants spread throughout 698 congregations.

By the adopted constitution, all the separate synods transferred their rights and properties to the larger group. The separate synods became districts of the Wisconsin Synod. The old Wisconsin Synod became three districts of the new synod—the Northern Wisconsin District, the Western Wisconsin District, and the Southeastern Wisconsin District. Minnesota, Michigan, and Nebraska also became districts of the synod. In 1918 the congregations in the Pacific Northwest became another district, and in 1920 those in Dakota-Montana became a district of the synod. These eight districts were the Wisconsin Synod for over 30 years. No new districts were added to the synod until 1954, when the Arizona-California District became part of the synod.

A Merger: Working Together

In 1889 Philipp von Rohr of Winona, Minnesota, succeeded John Bading as president of the Wisconsin Synod. Von Rohr was president when the federation of synods became a reality in 1892. In 1908 Gustav Bergemann was elected president of the Wisconsin Synod, and he became president of the merged synod in 1917. He served the Wisconsin Synod until 1933 and guided it through its formative years as a single church body. In his history of the Wisconsin Synod, E. Fredrich said of President Bergemann, "Muehlhaeuser founded the Wisconsin Synod. Bading shaped its confessional stance. Bergemann gave it its organizational form. Bergemann made the merger and then made it work."

President Bergemann

President Bergemann traveled a great deal to make the merger work. He reported to the 1919 convention that he spent only eight full weeks with his congregation in Fond du Lac. Very often his weeks were interrupted by travel, mostly travel by train. One of his trips took him to Yakima, Washington, to be present at the first convention of the Pacific Northwest District.

World War I and the Depression

World War I and the Depression created additional problems for Bergemann and the synod. When the war broke out, almost all church services and confirmation classes were still conducted in German. The war brought a kind of hysteria against all things German. Sauerkraut became liberty cabbage, and some states passed legislation forbidding the use of German in public gatherings.

In the Wisconsin Synod, the war helped accelerate the use of English. Yet many feared that the loss of German would spell the loss of our

Lutheran heritage. The English *Northwestern Lutheran* began publication in 1914, but the members of the synod preferred the German *Gemeinde-Blatt*. Not until 1939 did the subscribers to the English magazine outnumber the subscribers to the German one.

Once the war was over, the synod turned its attention to the needs of its worker-training schools. The seminary at Wauwatosa was badly overcrowded. Rather than build in Wauwatosa, in 1921 the synod resolved to acquire new property for its seminary. After a long search for property, the synod bought an 80-acre farm bordering the village of Thiensville, about 15 miles north of Milwaukee, for about $25,000. The building began in 1928. Professor J. P. Koehler became deeply involved in the planning for the new school, even neglecting some of his other assignments for the sake of the building. The new seminary was designed to resemble the Wartburg Castle in Germany and was built at a cost of about $350,000. The new home for Wisconsin Lutheran Seminary was dedicated on August 18, 1929, and remains today at the location chosen in 1928. The seminary building project was completely paid for by the day of dedication.

Dr. Martin Luther College (DMLC) in New Ulm, Minnesota, also needed additional buildings. The 1927 convention authorized the construction of a classroom building. The convention stipulated that "costs should not exceed the sum of $327,000." The new building became reality in 1928. As careful as the synod was to avoid a large debt, that's exactly what the synod got. The situation was complicated by the Depression and the establishment of Northwestern Lutheran Academy at Mobridge, South Dakota. The Wisconsin Synod entered the 1930s with a huge debt. Mission work suffered. Salaries were slashed. Graduates from the seminary and DMLC could not be assigned because there were no calls. It was a time of financial hardship for the synod and the country.

WORLD WAR I CALLS WELS MEMBERS TO WAR

In September 1917 at the age of 21, Herbert Holz left his father's butcher shop in Milwaukee and enlisted in the army. After basic training he was shipped out to France and World War I. He served with the 310th Engineers Headquarters Detachment. His job was to repair saddles and care for the horses. When saddle repair was slow, he and the others of his detachment filled holes left by bombs and artillery. He said, "I wasn't in any big battle, but I was kept busy filling holes. For that they called me an engineer. Others patched bridges so the cannons and food could go through."

Herbert Holz was a lifelong member of St. Matthew's in Milwaukee. While overseas he had no Wisconsin Synod chaplain, not even a Lutheran chaplain, but he did meet a Roman Catholic chaplain. For spiritual strength, Herb had to rely on his Bible and the letters and literature he received from his family and from his church back in Milwaukee.

He was discharged on July 9, 1919, and returned to the family meat-cutting business. In 1999 the French government honored all surviving American veterans who fought in France in World War I. Herb and the other veterans received the Chevalier of the National Order of the Legion of Honor, the highest award of merit offered by France. At the age of 103, Herbert Holz was taken home by his Lord to the glory of heaven.

A CENTURY

TOGETHER

THE PROTEST

In 1924 a group of students at Northwestern College in Watertown were disciplined for stealing. The discipline by the faculty was set aside by the college board. The case, at first, appeared to be a simple matter of a difference of opinion, but it sparked a protest that shook the synod. Two college teachers resigned, and their positions were filled by the board. Some objected to the college board's action, but the protesters could not change the opinion of the board. The difference of opinion festered.

Shortly after the incident at Northwestern, another case of discipline developed in Fort Atkinson, involving two elementary school teachers who objected to the moral conditions in American society during the 1920s. The teachers were suspended because they called their pastor a false prophet. At the June 1926 Western Wisconsin District meeting in Beaver Dam, a majority of delegates ratified the suspension of the teachers, but 17 delegates refused to agree. They presented a written protest and suggested that a bigger problem lurked beneath the surface. The situation was not settled. Instead, it only grew worse. At a pastoral conference near Wausau in September of 1926, Pastor William Beitz delivered a paper that expanded the conflict.

The paper generated a great deal of discussion and disagreement. Some felt that Pastor Beitz had correctly highlighted the lack of spiritual life in the synod. The two discipline cases—the students at Northwestern and the teachers in Fort Atkinson—seemed to support the contention that the synod, and in particular its officials, did not have the theological or moral courage to do the right thing. Others felt that Beitz' denunciations were too broad and sweeping. The clashes over his paper worsened. In July of 1927, Beitz was suspended from fellowship. Others were also suspended.

The Western Wisconsin District sought to settle the matter by asking for an official opinion from the seminary faculty. Under the direction of

Professor Koehler, the seminary faculty prepared an evaluation of the controversy. Although Koehler himself gave little time to the problem because of the seminary building plans, he did sign the document. Unfortunately, the seminary opinion served to add fuel to the fire rather than put it out. In subsequent events, Koehler withdrew his signature from the seminary document, which set the stage for a bitter clash with Professor August Pieper.

Professor Koehler

The results of this protest have lingered. Professor Koehler's service to the synod was terminated. He went on to write an important history of the Wisconsin Synod. A small group of congregations remains outside the Wisconsin Synod as the Protes'tant Conference, its name emphasizing the protest of the 1920s. It began publishing a periodical entitled *Faith-Life* that still appears every two months. Attempts to resolve the differences have not succeeded, and as late as the 1980s, two WELS congregations were troubled by issues relating to the protest.

JOINING TOGETHER
TO EDUCATE THE YOUNG

Since its beginning the Wisconsin Synod has been deeply committed to educating young people. In May of 1850, the new synod resolved that every pastor should "devote himself especially to the young and conduct a day school, and Bible and mission classes." In 1858 the synod numbered 17 pastors, 16 parish schools, 7 Sunday schools, but only 3 teachers. Pastors often doubled as school teachers in the early years.

Teaching was a job for men at the time. Large class sizes made teaching a difficult task. Teachers had to supplement their salaries by giving music lessons, working on farms, or writing for German newspapers. The first female teacher was the wife of Teacher Voss. She taught the lower

SCHOOL THEN AND NOW

In 1850 the first convention of the Wisconsin Synod resolved that every pastor should "devote himself especially to the young and conduct a day school, and Bible and mission classes." From the very first, elementary education was important. But schools have changed from those early days.

At first pastors often taught the children because there were few able and faithful teachers available. In those early days, athletic teams did not exist. Physical education followed the European pattern of stretching and bending—a form of gymnastics. Class sizes were generally large. Many schools had a single classroom with over one hundred children and one teacher. The largest classroom in the synod probably was at St. Jacobi

School in Milwaukee, with 123 students and one teacher. All the subjects were taught in German, and teachers were grossly underpaid.

When the government began to require that the three R's be taught in English, even our Lutheran schools slowly changed. Many resisted because they thought that the shift to English would signal a shift away from Luther and the Reformation heritage.

Today's schools have busy athletic schedules, computers, audio and visual equipment, dedicated teachers, and manageable class sizes. Lutheran education still aims to teach Christ and make the Savior's Word part of every lesson. By teaching Bible stories and Luther's Small Catechism, congregations prepare a new generation of Lutherans committed to the truths of God's Word.

grades at St. Mark School in Watertown, Wisconsin, from 1871 to 1875. But for many years the teachers in the synod's elementary schools were predominantly men. In 1947, one hundred fifty women taught in parish schools as compared with two hundred men.

Over the years, training the young has expanded to include not just elementary education but also high school. In 1903 a group of Wisconsin and Missouri Synod congregations began Milwaukee Lutheran High School. A Missouri congregation provided the space, and volunteers—including professors Koehler and Pieper of the Wauwatosa seminary—taught. Wisconsin Synod congregations have joined together to support other area Lutheran high schools. In 1926 a group of congregations in Fond du Lac created an association that began Winnebago Lutheran Academy. Associations have formed to support area Lutheran high schools throughout the synod. Today 21 such schools welcome students from California to Michigan.

Viola Zimmermann

President Gustav Bergemann was a key player in the formation of Winnebago Lutheran Academy. He claimed that he only reacted to the request of a young girl at the eighth-grade graduation service for his school in Fond du Lac. Viola Zimmermann stopped in the middle of her address and begged the congregation, "Please give us at least one more grade at our school." St. Peter's did provide another grade in the school, and soon after the association began the high school.

A NEW PRESIDENT

Over the years President Bergemann had more difficult problems to face, however. Because of the synod's huge debt, he had some sober words for the 1933 synod convention. In his report President Bergemann regretfully informed the delegates, "Under prevailing circumstances there could be no thought of an enlargement of our work. No additional mission programs could be undertaken. The number of parish schools also did not increase. Therefore the majority of this year's candidates for the pastoral and teaching ministry are without a call; even several from the past year are still on the waiting list."

Perhaps because of these bleak facts and because of the long and bitter protest in western Wisconsin, the delegates chose a new president. President Bergemann became Pastor Bergemann and served his Fond du Lac congregation for another 14 years. He continued as the head of the seminary board even longer.

The new president was John Brenner. Under his presidency the Wisconsin Synod retired its debt, undertook major building projects, and helped the synod remain firm in God's truth during the growing difficulties with the Missouri Synod and the Synodical Conference.

DEBT RETIREMENT

Only a few weeks before the Great Depression, the Wisconsin Synod carried a debt of $700,000. Part of the debt came from building programs, but the growth of the synod was not matched by a growth in the stewardship of giving. The debt had crippled the desire of most to conduct more mission work. One pen sketch depicted the synod as a locomotive pulling a string of cars marked as missionaries. The train was stalled because of a deep washout labeled "debt." The caption read, "Help us get rid of the debt so the synod can get going again."

It was as bleak as President Bergemann had reported to the 1933 convention. The 1935 convention wrestled with the problem but had no solution. On the last day of the convention, just as everyone was preparing to leave, a pastor moved to "retire our debt without delay." A New Ulm hardware man, Mr. Frank Retzlaff, who already had his hat on and was walking out the door, turned and seconded the motion. The motion passed by a large majority. In spite of the Depression, a determined effort at reducing the debt began. Together the congregations of the synod contributed to lift the crippling debt. By 1939 the debt had been reduced to just over $320,000. In 1943 it stood at just under $100,000.

During those years new mission work and building projects were stalled with the simple argument that the synod had no money. Once the debt was reduced, new mission work and needed building at synodical schools could begin. Members of the synod began to speak of expansion, even before the debt was fully retired.

WORLD WAR II AND CHAPLAINCY CONCERNS

When World War II began, Wisconsin Synod Lutheran Christians carried rifles, sailed ships, and flew airplanes to defend the United States. An estimated 22,000 members served in the armed forces. They were separated from their loved ones and from their congregations and were dispersed all over the world. The Wisconsin Synod cared for them through an extensive mailing program, through pastors near military bases, and eventually by sending its own chaplains.

Several problems prevented the Wisconsin Synod from participating in the government's military chaplaincy program. For one thing,

Pastor Erwin Scharf, civilian chaplain, and servicemen

the chaplaincy confused the difference between church and state. The state has a God-given responsibility to maintain order and establish justice. The church, on the other hand, has a God-given responsibility to proclaim the truths of God for the salvation of

Pastor Erwin Scharf

souls. The synod maintained, and still maintains, that the chaplaincy under the control of the government violates that separation.

Another significant problem is that a government chaplain must offer "Protestant" services and give burials to all. The synod had struggled to make itself Lutheran in the very beginning of its history. When the old mission societies had required its pastors to perform both Lutheran and Reformed services, the Wisconsin Synod said no. The chaplaincy issue seemed to drag the synod back to the vague Lutheranism of its beginning. After a study of the program, the synod again said no and chose to serve its members without using the government's program.

The conscientious objection of the Wisconsin Synod to the government's chaplaincy was not shared by others in the Synodical Conference. In 1938 the Missouri Synod began to use the government's program. The difference between the two approaches signaled the beginning of a long dialogue over doctrinal issues between the two synods. By the end of the war, more than one difference existed between the two synods, and the differences were discussed at the conventions of the Wisconsin Synod and the Synodical Conference often during the 1940s and 1950s.

CONTINUING IN HIS WORD

In 1950 the Wisconsin Synod celebrated one hundred years of history—a century of service to the Lord. Sermons, special articles, and anniversary services marked the event. A group of professors and pastors had been commissioned to write a history of the synod. They chose the title *Continuing in His Word*, which became the theme for the centennial celebration. The authors chose the title because it best described "the distinctive quality by which the synod under God overcame the doctrinal difficulties within itself, and later those besetting it from without."

In addition, the synod had authorized a special collection to begin the necessary building projects that had been delayed during the depression and war years. Soon a building boom took place on the campuses of the synodical worker-training schools. A new combination library-classroom building appeared at Northwestern College in Watertown. Michigan Lutheran Seminary added a classroom and administration building. Dr. Martin Luther College built its first dormitory for female students, Centennial Hall. Northwestern Lutheran Academy in Mobridge dedicated an administration-gymnasium building.

The delegates at the 1953 synod convention heard the report that just over $1.7 million had been spent on these projects. The new facilities helped increase enrollments, and the members at the same convention authorized a new collection for additional buildings: a dining hall in Saginaw and a dormitory-classroom building and dining hall at Watertown. A special gift from Meta Kilgas Michelson of Manitowoc made a new chapel at Northwestern College possible as well.

Chapter 6

TOGETHER
AS HIS
WITNESSES

Expanding the Home Mission Horizon

Florida and California

Together in World Missions

Stand Tall!

Africa and Japan

*Faithfulness to Christ
Means Separation*

1950	1952	1953	1955	1961
First synod services in California	*Missionary sent to Japan*	*Missionary team arrives in Zambia*	*First synod services in Florida*	*Synod resolves to break with LCMS*

EXPANDING THE HOME MISSION HORIZON

World War I had started the process of changing the Wisconsin Synod into an English-speaking church. World War II finished the process. As the synod directed its energies to eliminating its debt, some began to understand that mission work had changed. In the past the synod had followed the German Lutherans wherever they had gone. At the end of World War II, the Wisconsin Synod had congregations in 14 states, mostly in the Midwest. At the time, the Wisconsin Synod had eight districts, three in Wisconsin, and one each in Minnesota, Michigan, Nebraska, the Pacific Northwest, and the Dakotas.

Already in 1939 the synod had looked beyond the Midwest and authorized home mission efforts to begin in Colorado and Arizona. In 1942 both were "mission districts." Arizona was still part of the Southeastern Wisconsin District and Colorado a part of the Nebraska District. After 1950 greater job opportunities and better transportation throughout the United States created greater mobility. More and more people began to move from the Midwest to places where the Wisconsin Synod had no congregations. The changes in mobility created opportunities to establish new congregations.

FLORIDA AND CALIFORNIA

The synod wanted to move gradually and cautiously—no doubt because the lessons of the huge debt were still fresh in everyone's mind. Mr. Louis Ott, a member of the Michigan District's mission board, had other ideas. He had a winter home in St. Petersburg, Florida, and wanted the Wisconsin Synod to begin a mission congregation there. In February of 1954, he was part of the mission board team that headed south to explore the mission possibilities in Florida. Later that year he opened his home to the first missionary sent into Florida. On January 9, 1955, Pastor William Steih conducted the first public service in a school auditorium.

In the West new possibilities also called for expanded mission work. The synod had congregations in Arizona, as well as its "foreign" mission work among the Apaches, but had no congregations in neighboring California. That changed through the persistent requests of Mr. Carl Loeper. In 1950 two missionaries were sent to California. Both began work in northwest Los Angeles. The first public service was conducted on Christmas Eve, 1950.

Carl Loeper

Planting new missions requires resources. First, each new opening requires pastoral leadership. Second, it needs money. Once a nucleus is gathered and a congregation is formed, the people need a place to worship. Yet membership is small in the early stages of a mission. The small group cannot afford to pay the salary of its pastor, nor can it afford to borrow money to build. A large portion of the salary for mission pastors comes through the synod; that's why we are together—to help share the gospel and extend the Lord's church. In addition, the Church Extension Fund lends money to mission congregations so that they can buy land and build chapels.

The growth in mission congregations in the United States since 1945 has continued. Over the past few years, the WELS has done mission work in every state of the union. The *1998 Statistical Report* indicates that the WELS has congregations in 48 states. Only Rhode Island and West Virginia have no established congregations.

TOGETHER IN WORLD MISSIONS

For many years the only foreign mission work of its own the synod knew was among the Apache nation in Arizona. Yet the synod had participated in the foreign mission work of the Synodical Conference. In the early

41

STAND TALL!

His ministry began in Atmore, Alabama, and ended with a retirement call to Siloah Lutheran Church in Milwaukee, Wisconsin. Pastor Grigsby has left his imprint on all those who knew him. His comments provide food for thought for all those called together in Christ:

"Be what you are and deal with people. If someone calls himself white, he is still a person. If someone calls himself black, he is still a person. Every individual is a person, and if you remember that, you can deal with them. That has never failed me yet. In addition, take time to listen. Take time to really hear what the complaints are, what the problems are.

"But don't be afraid of your Lutheranism. When the missions came to Camden, they never once backed down from their convictions. Be what you are, and stand tall! But the key is that I saw people as people, and never worried about races. We treated every individual as a person, not as black or as white."

Henry Grigsby was born in 1906 and became a Lutheran when the Synodical Conference mission to the blacks started a school and church in his home town of Camden, Alabama. Although unable to read, his father memorized the entire catechism so he could instruct his children. Henry, the third of 13 children, turned down a baseball contract with the Kansas City Monarchs, the team for which Satchell Paige pitched, to become a Lutheran pastor. He completed his training at Immanuel Lutheran College in Greensboro, North Carolina.

years of the Synodical Conference, the synod supported the mission to the blacks, which was begun in 1877. The congregations of the black mission had gathered money to send for chapels in India and China and asked, "Why not share the gospel in Africa?" In 1927 a Nigerian tribe became dissatisfied with an interdenominational mission society and sent its best evangelist, Jonathan Ekong, to the United States for additional training at the Synodical Conference school in Greensboro, North Carolina. He returned to Nigeria in 1938. During Ekong's training at Greensboro, the Synodical Conference sent a team to survey the Nigerian field. Its report led to the adoption of the Nigerian mission work in 1936. The first permanent worker called from the United States into the field was William Schweppe of the Wisconsin Synod.

Missionary Schweppe (front and center) in Africa

The synod did initiate one overseas mission in the 1920s. After World War I, the peacemakers recreated Poland. Lutheran Germans became part of Poland and experienced hardships. Many in the Wisconsin Synod, some who had German relatives in Poland, sought to relieve the suffering by sending supplies to Poland. The concern led the 1923 synod convention to "undertake the mission in Poland with all energy." Unfortunately lack of money and men delayed the work. But the work did eventually begin, and a dozen congregations were organized. In 1939 William Bodamer, the missionary to Poland, was in the United States when Hitler's blitzkrieg and what followed made it impossible to return.

AFRICA AND JAPAN

The synod was not in a position to undertake any new mission work in the 1930s and 1940s; its attention was on reducing its debt. The end of World War II brought a renewed desire for mission expansion. Delegates

43

at the 1945 convention in New Ulm directed President Brenner to "appoint a committee to gather information regarding foreign fields that might offer opportunities for mission work by our Synod. When ready, this committee shall report the results of its study…to the Synod."

The Commission on Foreign Missions faced its share of difficulties, but in 1949 two men, Arthur Wacker and Edgar Hoenecke, were sent to Africa to explore mission possibilities. They traveled in a one-ton Dodge Power Wagon that had been refitted to be a house on wheels. The truck was painted white with a gold cross. Large black letters announced their purpose, "Lutheran African Mission—Exploratory Expedition." The two returned just before the 1949 convention and reported that Zambia, which was then Northern Rhodesia, offered the most promising field.

The synod did not act on the report until the 1951 convention. Then it resolved that the synod enter into foreign "mission work in the Northern Rhodesia field in Africa." Pastor and Mrs. Albrecht Habben and their lay helpers, Mr. and Mrs. Paul Ziegler, arrived in Lusaka in Zambia on June 5, 1953. In 1957 the synod authorized a medical mission project headed by Dr. Arthur Tacke. The synod also took one more step in resolving to place a man in Tokyo to care for the servicemen who were stationed there and to explore mission opportunities in Japan. Pastor Frederick Tiefel of Spokane, Washington, sailed for Japan in February of 1952.

FAITHFULNESS TO CHRIST MEANS SEPARATION

President Brenner had set the stage for the mission expansion by giving his attention to the synod's debt. The years after the 1945 convention could be considered the reawakening of mission zeal. Yet President Brenner also had other issues to worry about during his presidency—

serious issues. In 1938 the Lutheran Church—Missouri Synod had attempted to find doctrinal unity with the American Lutheran Church (ALC). Unfortunately, no doctrinal unity existed, but the Missouri Synod concluded that it was close enough to declare a partnership.

The delegates at the 1939 Wisconsin Synod convention protested. In spite of the protest, the relationship between the Missouri Synod and the ALC continued. The Evangelical Lutheran Synod (ELS), also a member of the Synodical Conference, joined the Wisconsin Synod in protesting the action of the Missouri Synod. Both felt that Missouri's agreement with the ALC came about only by ignoring real differences and soft-pedaling the truths of God's Word. Over the next years at every convention, the Wisconsin Synod discussed what it considered an erosion of the confessional Lutheran faith in the Missouri Synod. In addition, it shared its concerns at the conventions of the Synodical Conference.

Other issues arose such as chaplaincy and scouting. The Wisconsin Synod approached these issues differently than the Missouri Synod. The Wisconsin Synod called and sent its own chaplain to serve its members rather than be entangled with the government's military chaplaincy. Because national scouting organizations promoted earning God's approval by good deeds, the Wisconsin Synod established Lutheran Pioneers and Lutheran Girl Pioneers. The Missouri Synod chose other courses, and the conflict grew to a full-scale pamphlet war between the Missouri and Wisconsin Synods.

In 1953 the Wisconsin Synod elected a new president, Oscar Naumann. The rift between the Missouri and Wisconsin Synods did not heal. In 1955 the ELS declared that its ties with the Missouri Synod were broken. Also that year the Wisconsin Synod voted to "hold in abeyance" its final vote on a resolution to break with the Missouri Synod. The delegates wanted to give the Missouri Synod an opportunity to meet in convention and consider its position one more time. The resolution that was held in abeyance said, "Whereas the Lutheran Church—Missouri Synod has created divisions and offenses by its resolutions, policies, and practices not in accord with Scripture, we, in obedience to the command of our Lord in Romans 16:17,18, terminate our fellowship with the Lutheran Church—Missouri Synod."

Six years later, in 1961, the Wisconsin Synod suspended fellowship with the Missouri Synod by a vote of 124 to 49. It was a difficult time for all. Some felt that the Wisconsin Synod failed to be faithful to the Lord by holding the resolution in abeyance in 1955. For the sake of their consciences, they resigned their memberships in the Wisconsin Synod and formed a new church body called the Church of the Lutheran Confession (CLC). In 1962 its membership was 62 pastors, 60 congregations, and 8,992 souls.

Professor E. Fredrich, who lived through much of the turmoil, wrote, "For those who were Wisconsin Synod members in the middle years of the twentieth century and lived through the long struggle to maintain the Synodical Conference on its historic confessional foundations, the loss of the battles and of the war will always remain the most significant and traumatic episode in their own personal version of their church body's history. The struggle was long, stretching over a quarter century. The losses in cherished fellowships were large, touching personally most pastors, teachers, and lay families of the synod. The results could have been tragic in the extreme, as dire prophecies of the time from without and within loudly repeatedly proclaimed. That they were not was because the Lord of the church once again did all things well. It all began in 1938 and 1939 when Missouri issued its church union resolutions and our synod in the following year reacted sharply. It ended when the Wisconsin Synod in its 1961 convention broke fellowship with the Missouri Synod and when two years later it withdrew from the Synodical Conference."

Chapter 7

FORWARD TOGETHER

Joined Together to Work Together

Publishing His Truth Together

Into the World Together

Together in Home Missions

Continuing Together in Training Workers

Forward in Christ

1954	1959	1973	1983		1995
Arizona-California District added to synod	*Synod officially becomes Wisconsin Evangelical Lutheran Synod*	*South Atlantic District added to synod*	*North Atlantic District added to synod*	*South Central District added to synod*	*Martin Luther College begins in New Ulm and Luther Preparatory School begins in Watertown*

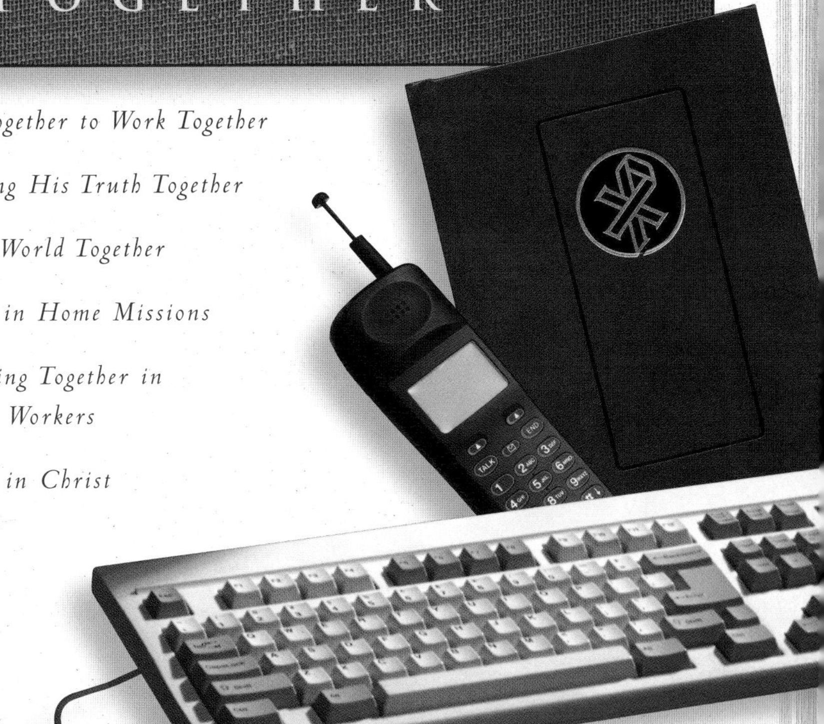

JOINED TOGETHER TO WORK TOGETHER

From the beginning Lutheran
Christians sought out one another.
John Muehlhaeuser, John Weinmann, and
William Wrede met at Salem Lutheran
Church in 1850 because they shared the same
confession and wished to strengthen one
another in the work for the Lord. From the days of
the horse and buggy to the days of personal computers,
many have gathered together to worship and to confess their faith as
disciples of Jesus. We are those the Lord has gathered together today to
be his disciples and his witnesses. We share a commitment to the truths
of God's Word as expressed in the Lutheran Confessions. We want to
remain faithful to the Lord of the church and to share his truth with others.

We do that individually. Each believer faithfully serves Jesus because
God has called him or her by the gospel. But no Christian is ever alone.
God also gathers us together as his people. Christians simply do some
things better together than they do individually. The history of the
Wisconsin Synod demonstrates that individual Christians and even
individual congregations have difficulty training future workers, carrying
on mission work in the world, and publishing Christian materials that
faithfully proclaim the gospel. We do these things better when we join
together than when we do them as individuals.

PUBLISHING HIS TRUTH TOGETHER

On September 1, 1865, the first issue of the *Gemeinde-Blatt* appeared. It
was a periodical intended to instruct the members of the congregations
of the synod in doctrine and practice. The early leaders believed that the
church paper would increase the sense of unity among the congregations—

that the congregations would feel more together. That periodical has disappeared, but the desire to print material for the congregations has not disappeared. The *Northwestern Lutheran* took over the role of the early German periodical.

In addition, the synod has seen a need for materials that are faithful to the Scriptures and committed to the Lutheran Confessions. In 1891 the Wisconsin Synod paved the way for a synodical publishing company. On October 8, 1891, Northwestern Publishing House (NPH) was founded. Over more than a century, NPH has printed the works of many of the synod's most important theological leaders. The printed pages from NPH have helped members of the synod to understand the truths of God's Word and to deepen their knowledge of Scripture and the Lutheran Confessions.

In addition to publishing the works of leaders like August Pieper, John Koehler, Carl Lawrenz, and Armin Schuetze, NPH has published a 41-volume commentary on the Bible. But NPH publishes more than theological works. Parish elementary schools and Sunday schools can turn to Northwestern's curriculum with the confidence that it will be faithful to the Scriptures and help them train a new generation of Lutheran Christians. When the use of personal computers became widespread, NPH also began producing materials to be used with the new electronic media.

INTO THE WORLD TOGETHER

President Naumann

When Oscar Naumann was elected as president of the synod in 1953, Wisconsin Synod missionaries had made a beginning in Japan and Africa. Before 1953 the synod had conducted "foreign" mission work in Arizona among the Apaches, for a short time in Poland, and together with other Lutherans through the Synodical Conference. The new initiative in the early 1950s launched a more aggressive foreign mission effort. In 1955 Edgar Hoenecke became the chairman of the synod's new General Board for Foreign and Heathen Mission. Pastor Hoenecke became a champion for world mission work; his desire for sharing the gospel with the world was deep, enthusiastic, and contagious.

Since that first step forward into Japan and Africa, the Wisconsin Synod has entered Mexico, Hong Kong, Puerto Rico, Taiwan, Indonesia, and India. Individual congregations of the Wisconsin Synod could not reach so far into the world with the gospel. Together they can. The foreign work of the synod has increased over the years. The *1998 Statistical Report* lists such new fields as Cameroon, Nigeria, Albania, Bulgaria, Russia, Brazil, Colombia, the Dominican Republic, and Thailand. In all world fields, that same report lists 3,245 children baptized, 1,562 adults baptized, and 2,566 adults confirmed. At the present time, we have 522 congregations and 72 mission stations scattered throughout the world.

TOGETHER IN HOME MISSIONS

After 1950 the synod took a more aggressive stance in sharing the gospel. Not only did world mission work expand, but so did mission work at home. In the 1960s Pastor Raymond Wiechmann provided leadership in home missions, and from 1968 to 1988, Pastor Norman Berg led the synod into an extensive mission planting effort that touched almost every state in the union by 1983.

The home mission effort created new districts in the synod. From 1920 until 1954 the synod had eight districts. Only the Pacific Northwest District was outside the Midwest. The growing number of congregations in Arizona and California led to the creation of a ninth district in 1954, the Arizona-California District. The mission work in Florida had the same result 19 years later. In 1973 the synod added the South Atlantic District, which included not only Florida but also Georgia, Alabama, Tennessee, and South Carolina. The synod had ten districts at that point.

Ten years later the home mission work in two other areas had expanded enough to make two more districts necessary. In 1983 the North Atlantic District included Wisconsin Synod congregations from North Carolina to Maine. In the same year, the congregations in Texas, Oklahoma, Arkansas, and Louisiana organized the South Central District and became part of the synod. Individual congregations could not have carried on such an extensive outreach and planting effort. Together they could, and the Lord has blessed the synod's efforts to share his gospel in the United States and the world.

CONTINUING TOGETHER IN TRAINING WORKERS

Once the debt of the 1920s and 1930s had been removed, the synod began an extensive building program on the campuses of its worker-training schools. Congregations needed more workers. The new facilities built in the early 1950s encouraged increased enrollment. The additional students meant more facilities. In 1959 the synod authorized a new

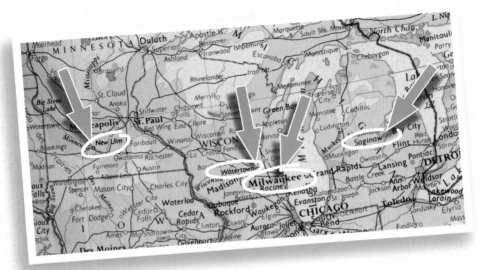

junior college in Milwaukee to help meet the need for the additional workers in our parish schools. In 1960 the junior college began its operation. By the 1969 synod convention, the need for an additional college in Milwaukee provoked considerable debate. Delegates at the 1969 convention resolved to merge the Milwaukee junior college with Dr. Martin Luther College in New Ulm. While the training of teachers for synod congregations was transferred to DMLC in 1970, dedicated members of the synod formed a new college in Milwaukee—Wisconsin Lutheran College.

Building on the campuses of the remaining synod worker-training schools continued. A new addition added library, science, music, and classroom space to Michigan Lutheran Seminary in 1964 and a dormitory in 1976. Northwestern College opened the doors of one new dormitory in 1967. The synod added a library to Wisconsin Lutheran Seminary in 1968. Dr. Martin Luther College dedicated Luther Memorial Union and an addition to its classroom building in 1968 and a library in 1971.

The Lord took President Naumann to himself in 1979, and Carl Mischke, the synod's first vice president, became the new leader of the synod. In

1978, the year before Naumann's death, the synod held a special convention in New Ulm and resolved to buy an existing campus at Prairie du Chien to serve as a new home for the preparatory school from New Ulm. The following year, 1979, the synod resolved to "discontinue the operation of Northwestern Lutheran Academy as a synodical institution." The new synod school, Martin Luther Preparatory School in Prairie du Chien, opened its doors on September 5, 1979.

The synod's worker-training schools remained the same until the 1993 synod convention in Saginaw, Michigan. The synod resolved to close Martin Luther Preparatory School in Prairie du Chien and combine it with Northwestern Preparatory School in Watertown, Wisconsin. The combined preparatory schools made it impossible for Northwestern College to continue on the same campus. The same synod resolved to move its pastor-training school to New Ulm, Minnesota, and join it with the teacher-training college there. The new preparatory school, Luther Preparatory School, and the new college, Martin Luther College, opened their doors in the fall of 1995. Both campuses saw major building projects to accommodate the shift in worker-training efforts.

In 1993 President Mischke decided to retire. The synod chose Pastor Karl Gurgel to take his place. Since his election the synod has adopted a new organizational structure in order to do the Lord's work together more efficiently. Part of the new structure called for the first full-time Vice President of Mission and Ministry. Pastor Richard Lauersdorf was elected to serve in that role.

FORWARD IN CHRIST

The consolidation of campuses and the restructure of the WELS organization close the first 150 years of our history. As we celebrate that past history, we note how the Lord has gathered us together and guided us. We may be a small gathering of believers by the world's standards. Even in comparison with other church bodies, we are small—only a little over 410,000 souls. Yet we share a commitment to be faithful to the Scriptures and the Lutheran Confessions. God gathered us to work together and blessed the faithful efforts of all those who have gone before us. We remain together to work as brothers and sisters in Christ and to proclaim the wonders of God's grace to all the world.

What lies ahead? What stories will be told about God's care of our small church body and our efforts to proclaim his truth? Perhaps another generation of believers will have the task of reviewing our current history and retelling its events. In addition, the next generation may stretch this story into the future and note whether we have remained faithful to our Lord and his Word. The Lord will not change. He will continue to call people by the gospel and give them strength to be his faithful witnesses. We can only remain faithful through his power. Because we are plagued by our own sins and weaknesses, we turn to him in prayer and ask:

> O Lord, let this your little flock,
> Your name alone confessing,
> Continue in your loving care,
> True unity possessing.
> Your sacraments, O Lord,
> And your saving Word
> To us e'er pure retain.
> Grant that they may remain
> Our only strength and comfort.

(Christian Worship 536:2)

ACKNOWLEDGMENTS

AUTHOR: John A. Braun

SPECIAL THANKS: Charlotte Sampe
                       WELS Historical Institute
                       Paul Burmeister
                       Kris Longendyke
                       Hare Strigenz Design Inc.

HISTORICAL
CONSULTANTS: John Brenner, James Korthals, Richard Lauersdorf

PICTURES: Courtesy of the collection of the WELS Historical Institute
                       at Salem Landmark Church (pp. 1, 3, 6, 8, 10, 15, 16, 18, 20,
                       22, 23, 30, 33, 39)
                       Carolyn Zeiger, MLS (p. 5)
                       MLC Library (p. 7)
                       St. Marcus Lutheran Church (p. 10)
                       By Gerry Koser, courtesy of WELS Mass Media (pp. 13, 22,
                       24, 27, 32, 50)
                       Robert and Carol Voss (p. 29)
                       Lorene Oldenberg (p. 34)
                       Ralph and Annette Scharf (pp. 36,37)
                       Carl and June Loeper (p. 41)
                       Tony Lustoff (p. 42)
                       Norbert Reim (p. 43)
                       John A. Braun (p. 53)

FOR FURTHER
STUDY: *Harvest of Joy*, a video history of the Wisconsin Ev. Lutheran Synod.
                       Wisconsin Synod, J. P. Koehler
                       The Wisconsin Synod Lutherans, Edward C. Fredrich
                       The Synodical Conference: Ecumenical Endeavor, Armin Schuetze